For Marit

Who is sure to
appreciate this excursion
into the oddities of
English usage.

Best regards,
Murray

CHRISTOPHER HOWSE

is Letters Editor of *The Daily Telegraph*
and a regular contributor to *The Spectator*.

RICHARD PRESTON

is masterminding an updated style-guide
to the *Telegraph* newspaper and
online media.

MATT PRITCHETT

draws the front-page cartoon for
The Daily Telegraph and has
won many awards.

She Literally Exploded

The *Daily Telegraph*
Infuriating Phrasebook

Christopher Howse
and Richard Preston

with illustrations by
Matt Pritchett

CONSTABLE • LONDON

Constable & Robinson Ltd
3 The Lanchesters
162 Fulham Palace Road
London W6 9ER
www.constablerobinson.com

This edition published by Constable,
an imprint of Constable & Robinson, 2007

ISBN: 978-1-84529-675-9

Printed and bound in the EU

1 3 5 7 9 8 6 4 2

Introduction

All over Britain each morning otherwise peaceable people are lobbing slippers or even half-finished pots of yoghurt at the radio. The occasion for their rage is one more intolerable act of mangling the English language on the *Today* programme.

We know this, because when the question of the most infuriating phrases came up in the Letters page of *The Daily Telegraph*, hundreds of readers wrote in with their pet hates and thousands more were posted online. Some readers confessed to early-morning radio rage.

It is not just the stuff that comes from the

mouths of politicians and commentators, with their 'Let's be perfectly clear', and 'priorities' and 'time to move on' and 'issues around'. All through the day we are infuriated by gangs of verbal muggers. 'You all right there?' asks the uninterested shop assistant after we have been waiting a very long time for an engrossing piece of stocktaking to be completed. 'How are you spelling that?' asks the woman at the other end of the telephone line once we have negotiated the endless pressing of numbers for unsuitably predetermined options.

At work, idiots expect us to 'touch base' and 'run that by' them again. In an apparently civilised restaurant, the waiter loses his senses by talking of 'pan-fried' fish and 'oven-baked' dishes and 'freshly picked' vegetables. Does he expect us to approve, for heaven's sake?

The greatest treason comes from those who declare that they know about words and are paid to put them before us: critics, authors and journalists. They write of 'iconic' and 'innovative' work and claim to give us 'sneak previews'. No cliché is safe from their eager grasp.

Provoked beyond endurance, we two *Daily Telegraph* journalists decided to compile this *Infuriating Phrasebook*, drawing on written and spoken insults to the intelligence from television, radio and the printed word. The title *She Literally Exploded* is taken from an overheard remark made without any awareness of its untruth and absurdity. An inability to distinguish between what is literal and metaphorical is a prime characteristic of the habitually infuriating phrasemaker.

Matt Pritchett, the brilliant cartoonist who has never committed a cliché in all the thousands of front-page jokes he has drawn for *The Daily Telegraph*, supplied the illustrations.

Christopher Howse
Richard Preston
London, 2007

She Literally Exploded

The *Daily Telegraph*
Infuriating Phrasebook

Absolutely *'Have you ever heard of the word Yes?' 'Absolutely.'*

Accenture A trade name beginning with a small letter and having a silly > sign above the letter *t*. See also *stupid trade names*.

Accountability An imaginary mechanism for delivering [*qv*] cost-effective, uncorrupted democracy.

Action Verb. *The target is to action 40 per cent of applications by 2012.*

Actual *In actual fact.* What other kinds of facts are there?

Actually Often a preliminary to an untruth. *Actually, I wish the Chancellor well.*

Actually   As an emphasis, like banging the table. *The dog was actually chasing me down the road.* See also *literally.*

Added bonus   *Easy access to services is an added bonus.* See also *value added.*

Advance warning   Not the kind that comes after the event.

Advert   Instead of *advertisement.* See also *invite.*

Affordable   *Luxury cuisine at an affordable price,* say the retailers hopefully. *Affordable housing* has proved a crock at the end of the rainbow.

Ahead of   Instead of *before.*

Aims and objectives   And *targets* and *goals*, no doubt.

Alarmed   *Warning: This door is alarmed.* I am terrified.

All-important   My *all-important* is so much more so than your *important*.

All right   *You all right there?* A patronising enquiry made by nurses to old ladies already humiliated by being addressed by their Christian names. Also used by shop assistants to customers who have been waiting a long time for service.

Almost   *Almost exactly; almost unique.* Is it or isn't it? See also *exactly* and *unique*.

Along the same vein   A bastard child of *in the same vein* and *along the same line(s).*

Alright   Instead of *all right. Alright* is simply mis-spelled.

Any shape or form   See *way, shape or form.*

Any time soon   Sometimes written *anytime soon.* It is when arch writers and broadcasters advise us not to expect things. See also *breath.*

Around   See *issues around.*

Arrive into   *The train will shortly arrive into Rugby.*

As   *As big as it was*, instead of *big as it was*. Once, we all happily said: *Patient as I am, I was irritated by Chris Moyles.* Suddenly newspapers and broadcasters say: *As patient as I am . . .* Why?

As far as . . . goes   An unattractive phrase made worse when the verb is mislaid. (*As far as school transport, we remain committed to a comprehensive service.*) *As for* is shorter and plainer.

Ask   *A big ask.* Sporting commentators' childish cliché for a difficult prospect. *For England to avoid the follow-on will be a big ask.* See also *watch* and *listen*.

Asterix   A French comic book character rather than a small star used in text.

As time progressed   Time doesn't progress; it passes.

At the end of the day   See *end of the day*.

At the top of the hour   See *top*.

At this moment in time   See *moment*.

Awareness   *Increase awareness of. We're seeking to increase awareness of issues around smoking.*

Awesome   An adjective degraded by overuse. The awe has evaporated. *This muesli is awesome.* See also *like*.

Baby   *'What's she had?' 'A little baby boy.'* A boy, then.

Back   *Northern areas won't be feeling too clever, with hail coming on the back of squally showers.*

Back   *Off my own back.* Used erroneously for *off my own bat.*

Back-to-back   Formerly referring to a terrace of houses backing on to another, similar terrace, but now used where *consecutive* is meant.

Bacteria   Used as a singular instead of *bacterium*. See also *criteria*, *phenomena*.

Ballpark figure   Derived from *in the ballpark*, referring to a baseball park; an American term for a rough estimate.

Barista (also **barrista**)   Coffee maker.

Barrier   An obstacle, the existence of which politicians like to deny. *There's neither a resource barrier nor a skills barrier holding back schools.*

Based around   Bases are at the bottom of things so something is based on something else, not around it. See also *centring round.*

Basically   *Basically, I disagree with everything you say. Basically, we need to talk.* See also *talk.*

Basis Used to form a cumbersome adverbial phrase instead of an adverb: *on a daily basis*, instead of *daily*; *on a voluntary basis*, instead of *voluntarily*.

Bear with me Panic-stricken plea, e.g. by cloakroom attendant who realises he has given your cashmere overcoat to someone else. See also *having said that*.

Beg the question *Wayne's bought Colleen an enormous diamond ring. Which begs the question, will he marry her?* No, it doesn't, it raises the question. To beg the question, a phrase borrowed from formal logic, means to use in argument an assertion for which there is no evidence other than the argument itself: *This book is rubbish because it's obviously without merit.*

BEAR WITH ME

Behalf *On my behalf* instead of *for my part. On my behalf, I'm 110 per cent committed to the project.*

Believe you me   More aggressive, less sincere version of *believe me.*

Be safe   An impossible instruction masquerading as good wishes. See also *take care, mind how you go.*

Best practice   The bedfellow of *a commitment to excellence.* See also *gold standard.*

Bet *All bets are off. As far as* [qv] *whether the Tories will cut taxes all bets are off.*

Be that as it may   Seemingly polite acceptance of another's view that implies *I am rattled but I am not going to give you satisfaction by agreeing with or denying your statement.*

Big ask   See *ask*.

Big up   Let us praise.

Bits   *Love him to bits.* Cute appendix that can water down the sincerity of the declaration: *I love him to bits, but . . .*

Blue-sky thinking   Species of daydreaming for which businesses are usually billed by the hour. Can lead to *thinking the unthinkable* or *saying the unsayable* [*qqv*].

Bored of   Pedants can get *bored with* or *by* pointing out this error.

Both   Instead of *either*. *Trains are not stopping at King's Cross in both directions.*

Bounce   Version of *trot*. *Arsenal have now won three games on the bounce.*

Box seat   Cricket commentators' cliché. *With Flintoff gone, India are in the box seat.*

Brains   *Can I pick your brains?* Usually *for a moment.*

Breath   *Don't hold your breath. The results of your blood test could arrive on Thursday, but don't hold your breath.* See also *any time soon.*

Business community   One of the many types
   of community [*qv*] that prefer to keep at a
   distance from fellow members.

By and large   Usually.

C. difficile   See *Clostridium.*

Can   *Can I leave that with you?*

Can   *Can I stop you there?* You have.

Can I get?   *Can I get a coffee with my sand-wich?* Help yourself.

Can I upgrade that for you?   Well, of course you may if it's airline seats we're talking about; but if you're offering to put extra salad in my sandwich, please don't bother.

Carbon footprint   I'm giving up smoking to reduce my carbon footprint.

Care *Care in the community*: eviction from a psychiatric hospital and abandonment without sufficient help to ensure proper medical treatment. It often leads to homelessness.

Care *In care*: kidnapped by unaccountable agents of local authorities and exposed to a life of ignorance, crime, addiction, sexual corruption and tawdry consumerism.

Carer Sometimes used of a child or spouse who looks after a sick or aged relation. Annoyingly used as an alternative to *parent*, to avoid seeming to be judgemental [*qv*] about kids [*qv*] who haven't got a parent or parents. *Students* [*qv*] *must have risk-assessment forms signed by a carer.*

CHALLENGED
ICE

Cashback   *Do you have a Nectar card? Cash-back?*

Catch you later   *Got a lunch. Running late. Catch you later.*

Centring round   *Management is meeting concerns centring round parking provision.* See also *based around*.

Challenge   *Sales are down for the seventh quarter running and we need to reduce the workforce by a third. I see it as a challenge.*

Challenged   'Incapable'. *This is an improving school with a larger than average proportion of academically challenged students.*

Charismatic   *The charismatic spokesman for the Welsh Lib-Dems.*

Classically trained   'Had piano lessons as a child'. *Unlike most boy band members, Lee and Jermaine are classically trained pianists.*

Clear   A phrase used by politicians evading a point. *Let's be clear about this.*

Clear blue water   What politicians hope to put between themselves and their opponents. A Boat Race analogy that works better for the Tories than for Labour, clear red water carrying unhappy suggestions of the foaming Tiber.

Clostridium *Clostridium difficile* is often written *C. difficile*, which should only be done after it has been established which bacterium we are talking about. The word *difficile* is Latin. Annoying people, including doctors, on the radio and television, and even in so-called real life, pronounce it as if it were French, like Lucille.

Closure Once described the fate of Midlands car factories; now a state of mind. *Residents claiming compensation said it was not the money they were interested in. They just wanted to reach some kind of closure.*

Comfort break An opportunity for going to the lavatory. See also *toilet.*

Coming *I see where you're coming from; I know where you're coming from.* The phrase is ambiguous, meaning either 'I understand you', or 'I can see through the prejudices of your approach.'

Commitment to excellence Synonym for poor service.

Community *Security community; gay community. The dog-walking community was asked to be on the lookout.* See also *care*.

Community leader *Police consulted community leaders before making arrests in connection with the rioting.*

Concerns *After the stabbing, teachers' representatives voiced concerns over classroom discipline.*

Concerted effort Whatever you do, don't try it alone. To work *in concert* means working with others.

Connectivity What joined-up government lacks. See also *joined-up.*

Continue on *On* is redundant.

Convinced Instead of *persuaded. The Bee Gees could not be convinced to take part.*

Coruscating Meaning 'sparkling', used mysteriously often as if it meant 'excoriating, flaying', in the context of criticism. A symptom of a dullard's desire to coruscate.

Crashed names   This phenomenon is produced by branding agencies, giving us monstrosities such as easyJet, eBay. There is a variant (Travelodge, Parceline) in which the collision has been so forceful that a medial consonant has been annihilated. See also *stupid trade names.*

Crescendo   *Reaching a crescendo.* A *crescendo* is a growing intensity which reaches its height at a climax.

Criteria   Used as a singular instead of *criterion*. See also: *bacteria* and *phenomena.*

Cult   *Cult artist; cult movie.* This word is a guarantee that most people will not like whatever it describes.

Cultured   *This footballer has a cultured left foot.* Note, it is rarely the right foot.

Debate   A period of quietness preceding the introduction by the Government of an unpopular measure. *We must have a national debate.*

Decimate   Used as if it meant 'destroyed'. Originally it meant 'to kill one in ten'.

Deliver, deliverable   Targets are often delivered, unless they turn out not to be deliverable. See also *solutions.*

Detrain   'Get off' or 'change'.

Diarise   *Let's diarise that.* It sounds like a drug for intestinal affliction.

Disenfranchised   No *-en-* required.

Diversity   An obligatory agenda that pe-
nalises those who do not seek multicultur-
alism. *Diversity issues indicate that your
grant for work with prisoners should not be
continued.*

Do   *Let's do lunch some time soon. I don't do
smiling. I so don't do Shakespeare.*

Do you know what I mean?   See *know.*

Doing nothing is not an option   This phrase
is often applied to nuclear power, bird flu,
bad schooling, immigration, crime, the
NHS, the railways, global warming and
the overstretched Army. Yet nothing is
done.

Don't get me started   'Don't provoke me, I might lose control.' *The kitchen's bad – and the bathroom? Don't get me started . . .* See also *list is endless.*

Don't go there   A warning not to stray into a conversational no-man's-land that may come under fire. *I know you're unhappy about the forsythia but just don't go there, OK?*

Draw down   Verb. *We shall draw down troop numbers further so long as circumstances allow.* It means 'reduce' but is thought to sound better. The metaphor seems to come from water levels.

Drawdown   Noun. The compound term possesses a higher degree of jargonisation.

E. coli   See *Escherichia*.

Early doors   A metaphor from early entrance to a theatre, now applied to the timing of an unexpected exit, particularly from a sports field, often leading to an *early bath*.

Embedded   *Embedded reporters* are journalists attached to a military unit during an armed conflict; they take part in an *embed*. The term came into use during the 2003 invasion of Iraq.

Empower   *We need to recalibrate the benefits system to empower unemployed people and liberate their talents.* A euphemism for getting people to *shake their ideas up*. Not to be confused with *npower*, a gas and electricity supply company. See *stupid trade names*.

Enable   A transitive verb increasingly used intransitively, and carrying a moral quality. *I found the session on accountancy and Pilates very enabling.*

End of story   Used as a self-contained sentence with no verb, in an attempt to shore up an opinion. *The accounts department reports to me. End of story.*

End of the day   'Eventually'. *At the end of the day we're all going to have to sit down and thrash it out.*

Enjoy!   An order issued by waiters or *baristas* [*qv*] after they have delivered yours.

Escalate Costs and tensions, in particular, *escalate*; attempts to *de-escalate* them often lead to accidents. See also *ramp up*.

Escherichia coli It should only be abbreviated *E. coli* once the writer has established which bacterium he is referring to.

Ethical Used as if it meant 'green'. By that definition, Pol Pot's killing-fields would have been fine as long as they were organic.

Exactly; almost exactly *Here's your change . . . it's almost exactly right.*

Executive decision   Nervous declaration of intent designed to bolster self-confidence in absence of one's boss. *Well, I'm going to take an executive decision – we're all going to Pizza Hut this lunchtime.* See also: *pay grade.*

FALL PREGNANT

Fair *To be fair.* The phrase, on the lips of politicians, indicates that they are going to be indulgent of their own behaviour or negatively critical of their opponents'.

Fall pregnant *She fell pregnant when studying for her GCSEs.* The implication of *fall* is that pregnancy is an accident like slipping on the ice, or something that happens naturally without any thought, as it does to domestic animals.

VERY SUPPORTIVE PILLAR

Feeding frenzy *The arrival of Wii consoles in Regent Street set off a pre-Christmas feeding frenzy.* The cliché is less lively than the leftovers of a piranha's breakfast.

Feel *I feel your pain.* You do not.

Feisty *The feisty 19-year-old broke back in the third set.* A cliché often applied to American women. In point of historical development it derives from the description of a kind of energetic dog. The feistiness referred to the animal breaking wind.

Fine dining *Guests can look forward to a relaxing weekend of top-class leisure facilities and fine dining.*

FIREFIGHTER

Firefight   As opposed to a sword fight?

Firefighter   A supposedly non-sexist replacement for *fireman*. It does, however, introduce a belligerent element usually foreign to the behaviour of firemen.

First invented by   The second inventor is deservedly less well known.

First lady   Laura Bush is the first lady of the United States and Aretha Franklin may be the first lady of soul, but Cherie Blair is not the first lady of the United Kingdom.

First name   A supposedly inoffensive alternative to *Christian name*.

First up   A gift from Australia.

Flagship proposal   Political proposals continue to be flagships while they are still afloat. Once sunk, they are left as unmarked wrecks.

Flaunt   More often used by mistake for *flout* than the other way round. Anyone can make a mistake, but some people ought to know better.

Flow *Go with the flow.* A rhyming invitation to unthinking conformity in taking the course of least resistance. Dogs and guns are notionally criminalised, but no effort is made to deal with dangerous dogs and gun crime.

Focused   Instead of *concentrating*. *He was focused on qualifying as a leisure consultant.*

For free   See *free*.

Frank   *To be frank*. A warning of dishonesty ahead. See also *honest*.

Free   *For free; absolutely free; buy one, get one free; free gift*. Something is either obtained *free* or *for nothing*. Gifts are free. Other qualifications of *free* indicate a certain cost.

Freshly made sandwiches   Everything is fresh at its making. See also *new-laid*.

Friendly fire   An established term, but none the more consoling to its recipients for that.

Front-loading   A piece of jargon borrowed from a type of a washing machine. Now: talking to people and making preparations before launching a political policy.

Fulsome   Used as if it meant 'very full' (*fulsome apology*) or 'generous': *He responded with fulsome praise of the chairman's contribution over the years.* In reality, *fulsome* means 'disgusting by excess of flattery'. See also *unequivocal.*

Functionality A vogue term indicating an approved but unstated quality.

Fun size Small.

Game of two halves   A sporting cliché no longer amusing even in jest.

Gender   Gender is a grammatical concept distinguishing masculine and feminine words. The biological distinction between male and female is expressed by the word *sex*.

Get-go   *The compliance team was up and running from the get-go.* An Americanism that seems to defy grammatical analysis.

Get my drift   A conversational marker inviting acknowledgement from the listener, like: *see what I mean?*; *right?*

Gifted   Verb. Gave.

Give 110 per cent   See *per cent*.

Give it up   *Give it up for Sugababes, live on stage tonight.* Nothing to do with giving up smoking. See also *put your hands together for*.

Give me a sense of   See *sense*.

Gobsmacked   A synonym for *surprised* often used by people seldom smacked in the gob.

Goes to show   Seemingly sage addendum to an observation, though it is rarely clear what is meant to be shown. *Taxes have gone up under Gordon Brown, which just goes to show . . .*

Going forward   *Going forward, the company will have to reassess its goals.*

Gold standard   See *best practice*.

Good   *I'm good*, in response to: *How are you?*

Go the extra mile   To work beyond agreed limits without reward for a company that puts the bottom line first. *Team leaders should motivate staff to go the extra mile.*

Gotten   Gains may be *ill-gotten*, facts *forgotten*, and people *misbegotten*. Otherwise *get* has got a shorter past participle.

Government money   And where does it get the money from?

Grieving process   Grieving is a process, like the living process, eating process and dying process, that does not require a pleonastic addition. See also *peace process*.

Ground   *Here on the ground. The mood among the troops is buoyant, here on the ground.*

Ground   *Hit the ground running.* See *hit*.

Ground-breaking   A dead metaphor for the cliché *innovative*.

Growing   *Growing profits; growing the business.*

Handed a fine   *Jose Mourinho was handed a £2,000 fine*, instead of *Jose Mourinho was fined £2,000.*

Hand-cut   Artisanal term often used to describe the manufacture of potato crisps and chips. Perhaps a health warning. See also *line-caught, pan-fried,* and *oven-baked.*

Hard-working families   Suggesting that mother, father and infants are all in paid employment, the wee ones up chimneys. Morally superior to bone-idle families, perhaps, in which the children read and draw.

Hard-wired Something that is built into a computer's hardware and so not easily changed is said to be *hard-wired*. Now used to describe any human behaviour that appears unalterable. *Let's face it, women are hard-wired to want Jimmy Choo shoes.*

Having said that A version of aporia, a term in rhetoric describing a rhetorically useful expression of doubt that may be feigned. See also *bear with me*.

Head, go head to head Meet. *Table-topping Fulchester and minnows Skegness go head to head tonight.*

Head up Verb, as in *He's going to head up a committee.*

Heads up A warning. *I just called to give you a heads up on next week's sales figures.*

Health and safety Two unconnected concepts brought together by the Health and Safety at Work Act, 1974, and now permanently joined in pursuit of the elimination of risk.

Hello Formerly, a neutral greeting, sometimes accompanying a handshake. Now pronounced as an interrogative with the second syllable heavily stressed and preceded by *like* to suggest incredulity at another's behaviour. *I was, like, hel-lo? She really thinks she's going to fit into a size 8 looking like that?* Also used with stage emphasis as an indication that one's interlocutor is dim, dozy and needs waking up.

See also *wake up and smell the coffee.*

Help us to help you Customer service clap-
trap, usually the preliminary to a request
to fill in a 12-page questionnaire, in return
for which there is the chance to win a
comb.

Here on the ground See *ground.*

Hero (when not) See *legend* and *you're a star.*

Hey What the heck, never mind. *But, hey,
it's Tuesday.*

Hi As a written address, especially in emails.
It goes with addressing strangers by their
Christian names.

History *The rest is history.* It seldom is.

Hit the ground running Cod military metaphor implying Parachute Regiment-levels of fitness and aggression. *When the alarm goes at 7, I like to hit the ground running with a shower, a banana smoothie and a bowl of Crunchy Nut Flakes.*

Holy Grail See also *Mecca.*

Homophobic. The prefix *homo-* means not 'homosexual' but 'the same'. So homophobes ought to hate or fear those the same as themselves. In general they hate or fear those who are different.

Honest *To be honest; to be perfectly honest,* often signalling the opposite. See also *frank.*

Hopefully *Hopefully, the doctors'll be able to stick that back on for you.*

How *How awesome is this list of annoying phrases?*

How may I help you? By omitting *how*.

Human resources Language, music, water, food, forests, minerals, application forms, felt-tip pens ... only some of which can be found in personnel departments.

Hurting *I am, you are, he is hurting.* For 'suffering'.

I   In sentences where the word should be *me*. *Between you and I. The present pleased my wife and I.* The error is no doubt impelled by manners. As children we are taught not to say, *Me and Billy went fishing*, but *Billy and I went fishing*. This conditioning leaves adults with a feeling that it is both rude and ungrammatical to use the word *me* after the word *and*.

Iconic   *The iconic Mulberry handbag.* Anything vaguely recognisable.

I don't do irony   See *do*.

If you ask me   And even if you don't.

I have to say   You don't, but you will.

I hear what you are saying   A favourite of Lord Reith's. On other lips it is rude without being authoritative.

I know where you are coming from   See *coming*.

I HEAR WHAT YOU'RE SAYING

I'll let you go now   But you'll buttonhole me later.

I turned around and said   A garden-fence phrase devised to inflate the role of the speaker in an anecdote.

I'm good   See *good*.

I'm like   See *like*.

I'm not being rude   *I'm not being rude, but I really don't like you.*

Impact on   Verb. *The wind farm is likely to impact on local wildlife.*

I'm so   See *so*.

In actual fact   See *actual*.

Inappropriate   Used by officials who want to blame people for behaviour that is not illegal or forbidden. *The patient used an inappropriate tone when raising issues around ward cleanliness.*

In care   See *care*.

Including   *A risk of showers including on the south coast.*

Inclusive   Consumer advertisements exploit the exclusive. Social engineers seek the inclusive. Cut-price travel offers say 'inclusive' without stating what is included.

In excess of   More than.

Innit *I'm bored of ice-skating, innit.* A meaningless filler which no longer performs the function of *isn't it?*

Innovative   A word of praise seldom specifying the innovation made. *An innovative artist, he gained recognition as the winner of the Turner Prize.* See also *new innovation*.

In regards to   Ugly amalgam of *as regards* and *in regard to*. Avoid all three.

Inspirational   A modish alternative to *inspiring*. Often interchangeable with *innovative*.

Instant classic   *Britney's second album became an instant classic.*

In terms of   Misused as if it meant 'with respect to'. *We have voiced our concerns in terms of childcare costs.*

In the loop   See *loop*.

In the wake of   After.

Invite   Instead of *invitation*. See also *advert*.

Ironically   Used as if it meant 'oddly enough'.

Irony   A word excusing television comedians
who laugh at fat, homosexual, disabled and
foreign people.

Is is   *The thing is is that postal services need to
diversify.* The repetition of the verb *is*
would be almost incredible if it was not
heard daily on the wireless. It is sometimes
introduced by *the problem*. The construction is probably an unconscious echoing of
grammatically correct forms such as *what
the problem is is that*.

Issue Has made a successful attempt to supplant *problem*. By keeping its old sense of 'matter, question' in reserve, it can bring a tactical fuzziness to sentences.

Issues around *We're facing issues around MRSA targets. There are unresolved issues around health and safety compliance.* A favourite of health workers and bossy officials.

It must be said It need not be, but you can bet it will.

It's not rocket science See *science*.

It would've been nice Passive-aggressive remonstrance. *It would've been nice if you'd told me there were no WMD before we invaded.*

Joined-up   Joined-up government should mean that part-time workers who care for sick or elderly relatives are not penalised when the minimum wage is raised. But they are. A joined-up transport system should mean that those who heed calls to leave their cars at home should be able to make use of public transport. But they can't.

Judgemental   Description of the faculty that prevents one's own criminal behaviour, but must not be applied to the foolish misdemeanours of another.

Jus   Gravy.

Key The noun has long been used metaphorically: *Study is the key to self-advancement.* The noun used attributively is bad enough: *We must engage with the key issues. Targets have been exceeded at Key Stage Three.* Used predicatively it is unbearable: *Integration is key.*

Kids, kiddies *Christmas is for the kids.*

Knock-on effect *A pay freeze could have a knock-on effect in terms of recruitment.*

Know See *do you know what I mean?*

Lady The lowest grade of peeress is a baroness, just as the lowest grade of peer is a baron. We do not call peers 'Baron' but 'Lord', and we do not need to call baronesses other than 'Lady'. A painful error is to call the baroness Lady Blackstone 'Lady Tessa Blackstone', for that would indicate that she was the daughter of a duke, marquess or earl, and no peeress in her own right at all. The BBC brings down a curse on the body politic every time it commits this *bêtise*, which it does very frequently.

Learning curve Always steep but seemingly always worth the struggle.

Learnt *The Nine O'clock News has learnt . . .* See also *reveal* and *understands*.

Least worst   Lesser of two evils.

Left-field   Term from baseball implying an unconventional position removed from mainstream thought, possibly derived from one of Chicago's baseball parks where a psychiatric hospital stood beyond the piece of ground in the outfield on the catcher's left.

Legend, legendary   *Housewives had a chance to see the legendary television chef in action.* See also *hero* and *you're a star*.

Less   Instead of *fewer*. *Seven items or less.*

Lessons must be learned   Pious denial of responsibility. See also *moving on.*

Level playing field   The venue for a *game of two halves.*

Level   *Take it to the next level. We're taking pizza delivery to the next level.* Not to be confused with a *level playing field* [*qv*].

Life-changing experience   There may be such a thing, but the phrase is invariably used bathetically: *Appearing on* Strictly Come Dancing *was a life-changing experience for me, Bruce.*

Lifestyle   A voguish alternative to *way of life.* Also used adjectivally: *Collagen treatment was her lifestyle choice.*

Lift children out of poverty   *Since this Government came to power two million children* *have been lifted out of poverty.* See also *pulled from the rubble* and *power.*

Like   A marker indicating that direct speech is being used in place of an adjective: *I'm like, 'Wow'*, instead of: *I was surprised. He was like, 'No way!'*, instead of: *He thought it improbable.*

Likes   *The likes of.* A pejorative term *(I won't have my daughter pawed over by the likes of you.)* now applied to geniuses or literary celebrities. *The gallery houses paintings by the likes of Raphael, Titian and Francis Bacon. It was a party more likely to be thronged by the likes of Ian McEwan, Jeanette Winterson and A.N. Wilson.*

Limited edition Marketing phrase of questionable honesty first used by publishers, print-makers and photographers to imply rarity; now seen more often on kitsch plates, chocolate wrappers, drinks bottles and pet food packaging.

Line-caught See also *hand-cut*, *pan-fried*, and *oven-baked*.

Line manager *Inappropriate* [qv] *behaviour should be referred in the first instance to your line manager.*

Listen *A difficult listen, a hard listen*; see also *watch* and *ask*.

Listen up An American cop-show exhortation adopted by middle managers when addressing their sales teams.

List is endless An indication that the speaker or writer cannot for the moment think of any more examples. *Barcodes on passports, security cameras in airports: the list is endless.* See also *don't get me started.*

Literally Distinguishes the literal from the figurative meanings of a phrase, but is now used at random as an intensifier or a synonym for *really*, by those with tin ears. *I was literally exploding with laughter, she literally ran a mile; it was literally raining cats and dogs.*

Little ones   Cloying term for *children* that carries an implied threat when used by advertisers. *Because your little ones deserve it.*

Living legend   A legend who is getting on a bit.

Local residents   *Local residents were up in arms [qv] at the no parking sign that appeared in Acacia Avenue.* While those living several streets away or in adjacent counties knew nothing and cared even less.

Locals   Socially, a rung below the above, with a suggested tendency to violence and inbreeding.

Loop *In the loop; out of the loop.* A definition conceived by the insecure to indicate inclusion in some imagined inner circle.

Loved ones At the necropolis in Waugh's novel *The Loved One*, the living are referred to as the 'Waiting Ones'. See also: *nearest and dearest*.

Love you to bits See *bits*.

Major A non-specific hooray word, meaning 'important'.

Managing expectations *In managing user expectations, utilise prototyping for user/machine interface and operational support.*

Math *You do the math.* An American phrase, as is betrayed by *math* in the singular. The invitation to work it out implies that the answer is obvious.

May I be frank? Prelude to brutal verbal assault. Alternatively, an ironic introduction to a minor disagreement. See also *I'm not being rude.*

Mecca *China has become a Mecca for palaeontologists worldwide.*

Meet up with   Not to be put up with.

Meet with   An Americanism as in: *It's been a pleasure to meet with you.* But it can convey predetermination to meet: *At seven a.m. we meet with the delegation from Ohio.*

Meteoric rise   Meteors go down, not up.

Methodology   An orotund version of *method.*

Mind how you go   A chirpily vulgar valedictory, but saner than *be safe* [*qv*].

Misattached phrase   Much favoured by *Desert Island Discs. Born into a suburban family, his showbiz talents soon became apparent.*

Moment *At this moment in time.* 'Now', for heaven's sake.

Momentarily A confusing Americanism: *Mr Rickenbacker will be able to see you momentarily* . . . Mmm, I was hoping for a little longer, having travelled all this way.

Move on What we're all encouraged to do in the face of adversity. Politicians, in particular, like to advise this in case we spot what they're up to. *There is an issue around [qv] mass murderers absconding but really, y'know, the time has come for all of us with an interest in the criminal justice system to move on.*

Multi-disciplinary approach A collision, e.g. of social workers, psychologists and police officers.

Multi-tasking   Ability to load a dishwasher while making a telephone call, supposedly the province of women rather than men. See also *up to my eyes*.

Must of   See *of*.

My bad   A phrase used to admit an error.

Nearest and dearest Or as BT has it: *Family and friends*. See also *loved ones*.

Needless to say Needless but not omitted.

Net *Net effect, net position*. An empty borrowing from the language of shopkeepers' accounts.

New innovation A pleonasm. See also *innovative*.

New-laid eggs Another pleonasm. See also *freshly made*.

Next up *Small and mid-sized businesses are next up for outsourcing and offshoring. Next up* is thought to sound more lively than *next*.

9/11 A phrase embodying American conventions of giving dates: instead of meaning 'the ninth of November', it refers to the eleventh of September.

No-brainer *Do the math* [*qv*], *this is a no-brainer.*

No problem, not a problem, no trouble, no worries Used in response to a request with which there was never likely to be a problem, or which it was the respondent's duty to perform.

Not on my watch Used assertively to reject a course of action for which one would be responsible. Also used dismissively to deny responsibility for action taken by another.

Nucular   *America is deeply worried by Iran's nucular weapons programme.* A pronunciation used by several BBC presenters and others who should know better.

Number   *The number you called is busy.* Worse: *The number knows that you have called.*

Of For *have*: *might of, must of, should of. I might of known it was you.*

Of See *bored of.*

Off of *Take your feet off of the table.* Or in the words of the Rolling Stones, *Hey, you, get offa my cloud.*

Oh my God An American expression of surprise, sometimes meant ironically, but to an intolerable degree used in reaction to unremarkable occurrences, such as meeting a celebrity. It is also handy for youngsters awaiting A-level results, because it can be shouted in response to good, bad or indifferent news. Usually said with one-second pause between each word: *Oh . . . my . . . God.*

On As in *Nightmare on Elm Street*. The English is: *in Regent Street, in Piccadilly*.

On a daily basis See *basis*.

On a team Used instead of *in a team*. It has not yet extended to: *on a club*.

One-stop shop *For all your mobile phone needs*.

Ongoing Instead of *continuing*. *Police enquiries were ongoing*.

On my behalf See *behalf*.

On the back of See *back*.

On the bounce See *bounce*.

On the rise   'Increasing'. *Figures for burglary fell but violent crime was on the rise.*

Oven-baked   One of a gaggle of menu words intended to convey wholesomeness: *freshly-picked, field-fresh, hand-cut.*

Over-arching   The cliché is often reinforced by its coupling with intention: *Your over-arching intention guides your thoughts and actions.*

Over-exaggerate   Don't: it over-eggs.

Pan-fried Instead of being fried in an old dustbin-lid. See also *hand-cut, line-caught* and *oven-baked.*

Parent Verb. *The Government unveiled plans for parenting classes in problem areas.*

Park *Let's park that idea.*

Passionate about *I'm passionate about salsa/ stamp collecting/ equal rights.*

Pauses Before giving an answer or naming a winner on television, announcers pause, as if this makes it more interesting. It is interesting already. The pause is just annoying bad manners.

Pay grade   Deferential method of avoiding awkward discussions at work. *'Will we be getting a Christmas bonus?' 'I'm afraid that's way above my pay grade.'* See also *executive decision*.

Peace process   The unwarranted suggestion is that negotiations with terrorists always bring peace.

Perceived   A weasel word, its meaning sliding between 'understood' and 'misunderstood'.

Per cent   *Give 110 per cent.* See *go the extra mile.*

Permeate through   *Through* is redundant.

Personal belongings   *Passengers are requested to take a moment to collect all their personal belongings before leaving the train.*

Phenomena   Used as a singular, instead of *phenomenon.* See *bacteria* and *criteria.*

Pick your brains   See *brains.*

PIN number   PIN stands for Personal Identification Number.

Place   A mental state, not to be found in an atlas. *I'm in a strange place right now.*

Planet Earth Lest we're confused with a
  meteor?

Please RSVP RSVP stands for *Répondez s'il
  vous plaît*. It is true that English has devel-
  oped a verb, *to RSVP*. But *please* is implied.

Positively *I was positively livid when I heard
  the news.*

Positive outcome The equivalent of the
  footballer's *result* [*qv*].

Post Instead of *after. Manufacturing in the
  West Midlands reinvented* [*qv*] *itself post
  World War Two.*

Potentially *The women held aloft potentially
  lethal rattlesnakes.*

Potential risk   Once the risk is realised, it is no longer a risk.

Power   Governments used to *come into office*. Now they *come to power*, or even *take power*.

Powernap   See also *zeds*.

Pre-book, pre-board, pre-order, pre-plan   In a world that is increasingly *time-poor* [*qv*], it is apparently important to get things done before you do them.

Premiere   Verb. *The new Nissan hatchback was premiered at the Milan trade fair in July.*

Prior *There is a traffic hold-up eastbound on the B3426, prior to the Bricklayer's Arms roundabout.* Should we care what happened before the roundabout was constructed?

Priority Any deficiency that needs righting is called a government priority. There is no limit to the number of priorities.

Problem *Have a problem with.* Used in two annoying ways. One is equivalent to a challenge to a fight: *I'm just nipping down to the pub. Do you have a problem with that?* The other is irritatingly relaxed: *Your girl-friend is staying over? I don't have a problem with that.* Note that the American construction *don't have* is preferred to the English *haven't got.* See also *relaxed.*

Product Where *service* is meant. *The Wolverhampton Family Theme Park Experience: a quality product at an affordable [qv] price.*

Pull all the right levers Levers are not often pulled, now that railway signal boxes are automated, yet the dead figure of speech remains popular with the business community [qv] to describe a favoured product [qv]. See also *push all the right buttons* and *tick all the right boxes*.

Pulled from the rubble *A five-year-old girl was pulled from the rubble by rescuers three days after the earthquake struck.* See also *lift children out of poverty*.

Push all the right buttons   A dull variant of the dull *pull all the right levers*. See also *tick all the right boxes*.

Push bike   A bicycle.

Push the envelope   To go beyond the bounds of precedent. A cliché derived from mathematics, concerning the boundary of a set of curves on a graph. The mathematical envelope was taken up metaphorically by aeronauts 60 years ago. When Tom Wolfe wrote *The Right Stuff* (1979), the metaphor was still alive. Now it is dead. Hardly anyone who uses the phrase knows what an envelope is or why it should be pushed.

Put your hands together for   See *give it up*.

Quality product   It is not specified whether the quality is good, bad or painful.

Quality time   Something to spend with a spouse or children. An excuse for depriving them of the quantity of time they are due. Leftover food is not yet called *quality food*.

Quantum leap   Literally the hop of an electron from one energy level to another. Electrons are very small, but the cliché is often intended to signify a big change or breakthrough. See also *step change*.

Quote   Instead of *quotation*.

Raft of measures   *The Government announced a raft of measures to tackle child poverty.* Also *a whole raft of measures.* Meant to suggest breadth but implies hasty assembly, using driftwood.

Ramp up   To increase. See also *escalate.*

Real   *In a very real sense,* in the jargon of theologians: *not in a real sense at all, but metaphorically.*

Real world   *You wouldn't be able to get away with that in the real world.* A cosmology adopted by those who wish to establish the grittiness and realism of their attitude. See also *ground* and *there.*

Recognise   *I don't recognise those figures. I don't recognise that phrase.* Politicians have decided that they can get off the hook by declaring an inability to recognise an unwelcome statistic or a quotation from a previous statement. Such an inability would for anyone else indicate mental debility and perhaps senile decay.

Redated   Meaning 'delayed'. *Your operation has been redated.*

Reduces the appearance of wrinkles   This phrase raises complicated and time-consuming ontological questions; in considering them, one might ask whether a barber reduces the appearance of hair.

Regular   Small.

Reinvent the wheel   *We do not need to reinvent the wheel here. We already have mechanisms in place for local accountability* [*qv*].

Reinvent yourself An undertaking imagined to be easy by those with no well-formed personality. *After flirting with student Marxism he reinvented himself in the Nineties as a frontrunner in the ecological movement.*

Relaxed Unconcerned. *David's really relaxed about the drug-taking allegations.* See also *problem.*

Renewables Formerly, it was mostly library books that were *renewable*; then it became the preferred characteristic of energy sources, so that the wind itself, because it blows regularly, acquired the label of *a renewable.* See also *sustainable.*

Respect In gang culture, fear of violence. In government policy the name of an agenda.

Result   Used instead of *a win*. *It's a hard match to predict but we're really hoping for a result at Sunderland on Wednesday.*

Reveal   *The BBC can reveal . . .* That is rather what we expect it to do when we're listening to the news. See also *learnt* and *understands*.

Reverend   *The Reverend Clark was left unconscious by the assailants.* If a clergyman is called the Reverend James Clark, he is to be referred to subsequently as Mr Clark, or Fr Clark if that is what he prefers. And while we're on the subject, not all clergymen are vicars. Some are rectors and some neither.

Revert   Misused as if it meant 'report back'. *After finalising costings revert to me with a proposal.*

Revert back   *Back* is otiose.

Revised fares   They've gone up.

Revisit   Used to mean 're-examine'.

Rising to a crescendo   See *crescendo*.

Risk of showers   *There's a fifty per cent risk of showers in the Midlands, so don't forget your brolly.*

Road map   A road map shows connections between places. The phrase is misused in referring to an itinerary leading to an unknown destination. See also *peace process*.

Robust   Policies are always robust, and robust defences are put up. Which is more robust, a policy or the defence of a policy under attack for its weakness?

Rollercoaster ride   A metaphor claiming excitement for activities that sometimes lack it: *Painting the garage by Monday was a real rollercoaster ride.* Also used as a stale image of things that go up and down, such as the stock market.

Rolling programme   *Also known as the Forward Plan, the Rolling Programme of key decisions contains information about issues on which the Council will be making a decision in the future –* notice from Stevenage Borough Council.

Roll out   Policies are rolled out, as if they were carpets. They are less easy to roll up again.

Run that past me again   'Sorry, I wasn't listening.'

Safe   A word describing an illusory quality of invulnerability mistaken for a moral virtue: e.g. *safe sex*.

Saving the planet   Remembering to turn off your laptop before driving to the supermarket.

Say the unsayable   A challenge unfortunately embraced all too frequently. See also: *think the unthinkable*.

Science   *It's not rocket science.* This seems to have ousted *It's not brain surgery.*

Sea change   An arresting image used by Shakespeare, now dully applied to change of any kind.

Sense   *Give me a sense of how this is going to pan out.*

Sense   *There's a sense in which.* A late-night arts show affectation, perhaps a development of the theologian's *in a very real sense.* See also *real.*

Service provider   A company without whom one cannot use the Internet or email. When something goes wrong, service is not a notable element in its response.

Serving suggestion   On the label of a prepared meal, a warning that the plate, tablecloth, and accompanying boar's head shown in the picture are not included in the small plastic container.

Should of   See *of.*

Showcase   Verb. *The weekend is designed to showcase some of the brightest talent in the north-east.*

Sides   Used by waiters to denote vegetables.

Signature dish   Something a cook is known
   to be able to make satisfactorily.

Silos   A vogue term for government departments that do not communicate with each
   other. See *joined-up*.

Silverware   Sporting trophy.

Sing from the same hymn-sheet, or **hymn-
   book**   A tired image of party unity.

Situation   *Wolverhampton is in an ongoing
   skills-shortage situation. Situation* is usually
   redundant. Unusually, for an infuriating
   phrase, its use has decreased from the epi-
   demic noted in the 1970s.

SILVERWARE

Skills gap Inability.

Sneak preview The preview is not sneaky at
all, but to say it is a sneak preview makes it
sound more desirable.

So *I'm so not interested. You're so* Gardeners'
Question Time.

Solutions These can be delivered [*qv*] by businesses. *Delivering integrated nutritional solutions* = cooking.

Sorted An aggressive alternative to getting things *sorted out*. Characters in soap operas shout: *Get it sorted.* The BBC recently screened a serial about 'the lives and loves of postmen' called *Sorted.* It was a play on words.

Source Verb, meaning 'to buy'. *All of our sauces are sourced locally.*

Space A room. *It's a great space.* Also: *I don't have room for a relationship right now, I need my space.* See also *place.*

Spelling *And how are you spelling that?*

Spiral out of control *Residents feared that costs for the leisure complex would spiral out of control.* When aeroplanes spiral out of control they go downwards. Spiralling costs seldom do the same. See also *escalate*.

Spoil him rotten *What kid doesn't get into trouble? When he's around I spoil him rotten.*

Stakeholder A word fostered by politicians to suggest that voters own a share of the body politic, instead of having had it confiscated through taxation. Oddly enough, *stakeholder* previously denoted a participant in a gambling session.

State of the art New.

Station stop When one of the constant

loudspeaker announcements on a train wakes you up, if it is not to tell you that the buffet is closing, it is to make it clear that Rugby is the station at which the train stops next, not the one it is whizzing through, in case you were thinking of trying to get off there. See also *train station*.

Step change This metaphor is so dead that many people think it refers to a marching column changing step. In fact the figure derives from mathematics. The metaphor means that the change is not slight or one of quality, but a sharp movement up or down a level. In reality, the word *change* attracts the qualification *step* as often it does the word *sea* [*qv*], with no greater effect. See also *quantum leap*.

Step up to the plate A cliché from baseball, an American game. The plate is where batting is done. *It's high time consumers stepped up to the plate and confronted their carbon footprints.*

Still to come A phrase employed by broadcasters, usually. Pronounced *stiltercome.*

Student Used instead of *pupil.*

Stupid trade names Trade names become ever more unmemorable and dislocated from the business they represent. *Consignia* for the Post Office was a prize example; if anything, it suggested a left-luggage office. *Diageo* is another. Some are of doubtful pronunciation: *Wii.* Some attempt to pass themselves off as a series of capital letters: *SAVE*. Some eschew capitalisation: *npower, accenture. Accenture* also has a silly diacritical mark > over it. Many entail crashed names, such as *easyJet* (also with small initial letter, like *eBay*). See *crashed names.*

Supportive   An entry in the lexicon of empathy. *I really appreciated how supportive care workers were during the remand period.*

Sustainable   A necessary qualification for development or resources. See also *renewables.*

Table water   Comes in a bottle, at a price. See also *water*.

Tad   *The main course was a tad heavy.*

Take care   Although this phrase bears a close analogy to *beware*, it is regarded as a friendly valedictory rather than a threat. See *safe*.

Take on board   *We need to take on board the input from marketing on this one.*

Talk   *We need to talk.* In 'relationships' this spells trouble. In business it need mean no more than another vacuous meeting ahead.

Talk the talk   *Don't talk the talk if you can't*

walk the walk. Roughly equivalent to: *Put your money where your mouth is.* The jingle of *talk the talk* and *walk the walk* has gained them a vogue usage as if their repetition were in itself amusing.

Talk to the hand   *Talk to the hand, because the ear's not listening.* A piece of studied rudeness popularised by American television in the 1990s, now often used *ironically* [*qv*].

Task   Verb, to issue an order or request. *John's been tasked with implementing his homework.*

Terminate   *We will shortly arrive* [*qv*] *into Victoria Station where this train will terminate.* The journey might terminate but the train will live to make the return trip.

There *Out there.* The real world [*qv*] as seen from the broadcaster's studio.

There *There you go.* The triumphant cry of a shop assistant at the completion of an unhelpful encounter with a customer.

There's a sense in which See *sense.*

The rest is history See *history.*

They, them, their Instead of *he, him, his/she, her.* A failure of pronouns to agree with verbs is a glaring grammatical error, but is embraced to avoid specifying sex: *The caller withheld their number.*

Thing *The thing is is.* See *is is.*

Think *Think outside the box; blue-skies thinking.* Desiderata for businessmen and politicians, except when the original thoughts clash with the corporate culture.

Think the unthinkable An invitation extended by the Government in 1997 to Frank Field as Minister for Welfare Reform. When he succeeded he was dropped from his ministerial post. See also *say the unsayable*.

This is she Facetious answer on the telephone by the woman asked for.

Thoughts and prayers *Our thoughts and prayers are with you at this difficult time.* Usually untrue, unless said by a clergyman.

Tick all the right boxes See also *pull all the right levers; push all the right buttons.*

Time-challenged   Busy.

Time period   It is possible to have a *space of time*, but *period* happily expresses time without the uncalled-for aid of the word itself.

Time-poor   Busy but rich.   Liable to ask a secretary to buy a birthday present for his wife.

Tipping point   Formerly *turning point*. Malcolm Gladwell wrote a book of popular sociology called *The Tipping Point* in 2000, in which the phrase shared something of the meaning of *critical mass*.

To be fair   See *fair*.

To be perfectly honest   See *honest*.

Toilet A shibboleth for the middle classes, among whom *lavatory* remains the correct euphemism.

'I'll wait for a lavatory'

Top *At the top of the hour.* A dully obvious metaphor taken from clocks.

Top-slicing The removal of a percentage of the budgets for several bodies to pay for a centralised operation. *Primary care trusts are being top-sliced to finance the regional centre.* The phrase is sometimes misused to mean *cut*, or to convey no discernible sense.

Top story On television news, the massacre, disaster or crime that has won the competition to be mentioned first in the bulletin.

Total Adjective. Usually an empty emphatic: *The government response is a total betrayal of public sector workers.*

Touch base To talk to someone briefly in the

hope that an idea might emerge. An approved metaphor in business management circles, derived from the game of baseball.

Trademark Adjective. *Paul McCartney's trademark two-finger salute.* A dead metaphor for *habitual.*

Trade names See *stupid trade names.*

Train station A suddenly popular substitute for *railway station*, or just *station*, which have served well enough for a century and a half. The model is *bus station* and the origin is American. See also *station stop.*

Trial Verb. Try out.

24/7 No relation to *9/11* [*qv*].

Unchartered   Yachts that are moored at St Tropez awaiting the arrival of P. Diddy, Posh and Beyoncé may be *unchartered*; waters that haven't been mapped are *uncharted*.

Understands   *The BBC understands that . . .* A coy signal of hoped-for exclusivity. See also *reveal* and *learnt*.

Unequivocal   A description of one's own apology. See also *fulsome*.

Uni   A former polytechnic.

Unique   Usually qualified with *almost*.

Up and running   *We had the literacy hour up and running with sentence-level objectives for all Key Stage 2 students.*

Upcoming   *Preparations were ongoing for the upcoming telecoms franchise auction.*

Up for grabs   *Places on a university course in charity administration were up for grabs yesterday.*

Up in arms   *Mums in Leicester were up in arms at the closure of a council-run creche.*

Up to my eyes   *I'd love to take on the monthly compliance figures, but I'm up to my eyes with the work-flow spreadsheets.* See also *multi-tasking.*

Up until   Instead of *up to* or *until. Charlotte retained the demeanour of an angel up until the day she moved out to live with her boyfriend.*

Value added   *Milk producers going into organic cheese can market a value added product.*

Vast majority   Statistical lifebuoy grabbed at by drowning politicians. *Look, the vast majority of the public know why we're doing this and trust us to do it.*

Very much so   Try: *Yes.*

Vibrant   Usually paired with *dynamic* in government-funded attempts to persuade the public that an urban area is an interesting rather than dangerous place in which to live.

Victims of our own success   We were cocky. And we still are.

Wake up and smell the coffee   See also *hello*.

Wake-up call   Once, a telephone service offered by hotel receptionists; now, an all-purpose portent: *I was so off my face I don't know how I got home . . . It's a real wake-up call.*

Walking wounded   Specious military metaphor that conjures images drawn from Wilfred Owen but is more likely to be applied to the survivors of a company redundancy programme or a bruising budget meeting. See also *hit the ground running*.

Walk the walk   See *talk the talk*.

Watch   *A hard watch, a challenging watch,* of a film or television programme. See also *ask* and *listen*.

Water *Would you like some water for the table?* 'The table's fine, thank you; we'll drink the water.'

Way, shape or form A favourite of Tony Blair's. *The Government has no plans to do so in any way, shape or form.* An example of excessive denial.

Well *She was well fit.*

Wellness Since *health* has been appropriated by the *health and safety* [*qv*] industry, this is the term coined by nutritionists, fitness trainers and wholefood retailers to fill the gap.

Whatever A reaction suggesting open-mindedness or indifference. Sometimes used as the last in a list of selections: *I'll have bacon in there, lettuce, tomato, whatever* . . . More frequently an all-purpose single-word response to an unwelcome question or instruction. Parent: *If you don't come downstairs right now, I'm going to put your iPod in the dustbin.* Child: *Whatever* . . . May be a contraction of *Whatever floats your boat.*

What's not to like? What's not to wear? What's not to eat? What's not to loathe?

What's your take on . . . Invitation to dress up an unresearched opinion as fact.

Which part of 'no' don't you understand? Prolix attempt at establishing authority that succeeds only in being rude.

WINDOW OF OPPORTUNITY

Whole raft See *raft of measures.*

Window of opportunity Opportunity.

With (all due) respect Genuflection barely concealing the desire to force an interlocutor's head through a closed window.

Woodwork Crossbar.

Work colleagues They keep more regular hours and generally dress more tidily than the domestic version.

Work-life balance It must be maintained.

Workplace Where safety is to be striven for. Formerly: *at work.*

Workstation   Once it has been *assessed*, safety
is assured.

World-class   *We offer world-class solutions for
all your parking needs.*

-y *Crispy, pointy, stripey,* etc, rather than *crisp, pointed, striped.* A habit of speech encouraged by watching children's television programmes.

Year on year Compared with a year earlier. See *back to back.*

You do the math See *math.*

You know what? Yes.

Your call is important to us Inherently untrue, since the message is delivered by a machine.

You're a star Excessive and therefore patronising term of thanks for the performance of a routine duty. See also *legend* and *hero.*

Your guess is as good as mine   Irritating invitation to share in another's ignorance and incompetence, e.g., at the airport: Q. *Do you think there's any chance our baggage will arrive by the weekend?* A. *Your guess is as good as mine.*

Zeds   *I need to catch up on some zeds.* A longer version of a *powernap*.